Contents

1
Camping

Sam and Liz were on holiday.
They were camping.

It was Sam's idea.
Liz didn't like camping much.
But it was the only holiday they could afford.

They had found a cheap campsite near the sea.
It was just a field with a few tents in it.
There was a toilet and washroom.
But it was pretty basic.

Liz was already fed up by day two.

'There's nothing to do here,' she said.
'No bar. No restaurant.
No disco. No shows.
It's boring.'

'There's nature,' said Sam.
'Trees and fields and birds.
Fresh air and green grass.
Don't you just love it?'

'No, I don't,' said Liz.

'There's the beach,' Sam suggested.

'I'm talking about the evenings,' Liz replied.
'There's nothing to do in the evenings.
I wish we were in a hotel.'

'We can't afford a hotel,' said Sam.

'Don't I know it!'

'I know,' said Sam.
'Let's walk into town tonight.'
The little seaside town was about
three miles away.

'Oh great,' said Liz sarcastically.
'A three mile walk.
Then a three mile walk back
in the dark.
That's what I call a great night out.'

'Do you want to go or not?'

'Oh, all right,' answered Liz.
'Anything to get out of this field.'

2

The Theatre

They got into town about 7 o'clock.
It was a small town.
There wasn't much going on.
There were a few shops,
but they were all closed.
A seafront, where the wind blew fiercely.
A couple of pubs.
A small, run-down theatre.

'Let's go to the pub,' said Liz.

'Wait a minute,' Sam cried.
'Look at that!'
He pointed at the theatre.
A poster outside said:

THE GREAT POZZO.
FOR ONE WEEK ONLY.
HE'S MAGIC!

'What about it?' said Liz.

'It's a magic show.
Don't you want to go?' Sam asked.

'No, not really,' said Liz.
'I'd rather go to the pub.'

'We can't stay in the pub all evening,'
said Sam.
'We can't afford it.
Let's go and see the magic show first.
Look, it's only five pounds.
We can have a drink afterwards.'

'Oh, all right,' said Liz.
'If we must.'

Sam took her hand.
They went into the little theatre together.

3

'Good isn't the Word!'

Inside the theatre, it was dark and gloomy.
There were old, faded posters on the walls.
There was a smell of damp.
A little old woman sat
in the tiny ticket office.
She looked up when Sam and Liz came in,
as if she had been waiting for them.

'Two for The Great Pozzo, please,' said Sam.

'That's ten pounds,'
said the old woman in a creaky voice.
'The show starts in five minutes.'

'Is it good?' asked Liz.

The old woman gave a creaky laugh.
'Good isn't the word!'

Sam and Liz went through an arched
doorway into the small theatre.
A faded red curtain hung down
in front of the stage.
There were rows of shabby red velvet seats.
Most of them were empty.

'I wish we'd never come,' whispered Liz.

'Ssh,' said Sam.
'Give it a chance. It may be really good.'

There was a burst of tinny music
over the sound system.
Drums and trumpets, slightly off key.
It sounded so feeble, Liz wanted to laugh.

'Ladies and gentlemen,' said a voice,
'At last, the moment you've
all been waiting for . . .
The Great Pozzo!'

One of the curtains opened.
After a pause, the other one opened too.
The Great Pozzo shuffled on to the stage.

4

The Great Pozzo

The Great Pozzo was a tall, thin old man.
He was wearing a black cloak
and a pointed hat, like a wizard's.
His hair was white
and his eyes were dark and deep-set.
He had a slight stoop.
He looked very tired and ill.

'Ladies and gentlemen,' he said.
His voice was high and weak.
He sounded out of breath.
'I am the Great Pozzo.
Tonight, I am going to show you
some magic.

Not tricks. Real magic.'

He smiled.
Then the smile disappeared.
He clutched at his chest in pain.

'Do you think he's all right?'
whispered Sam.
'He looks very ill.'

The Great Pozzo heard Sam.
'I'm perfectly all right,' he said sharply.
'Nothing wrong with me.
A slight pain,
but now it's gone.
On with the show.'

He picked up a top hat
from the table in front of him.
'What do you think is in here,
ladies and gentlemen?

What would you expect to find in a
magician's hat?'

'A rabbit!' someone called out.

'Well, let's see,' said the Great Pozzo.
He showed the inside of the hat
to the audience.
It looked empty.
He turned the hat upside down.
He shook it.
He poked his wand inside.
'No rabbit there,' he said.
'Wait a minute – what's this?'

He put his hand in and pulled out
a large, live lobster.
A few people clapped.

'A lobster, ladies and gentlemen!
That's my supper sorted out.'

The lobster feebly waved its claws at him.
Pozzo put the lobster back in the hat.
'And now, ladies and gentlemen,
for my next trick . . .'

5

'For my Next Trick . . .'

_____

'For my next trick, ladies and gentlemen,
I will make the devil appear!
Yes I will. Old Nick himself.
Look, he lives in this box.'

The Great Pozzo picked up a wooden box.
There was a picture on it
of a grinning red devil with horns.
'Are you in there, Old Nick?
Knock once for yes and twice for no!'

A loud, knocking sound came from the box.
'Ah!' said the Great Pozzo.
'He's in there!

Well, Mr Devil,
why don't you come out and show yourself?
The audience would like to see you.
Wouldn't you, audience?'
One or two people mumbled 'Yes'.
Suddenly, the lid of the box flew open.
A little red devil stuck its head out.

It jumped on to Pozzo's hand.
It was an ugly little thing –
wet and slimy, with horns and a long tail.
For one second it stood there.
Then it jumped back into the box,
and slammed the lid shut.

The audience was shocked and silent.
Sam wondered what the creature was.
It must have been some kind of model.
But it did look very real, he thought.

'So, there we have it, ladies and gentlemen
–the devil! Let's give him a big hand!'

Nobody clapped. A few people
shifted nervously in their seats.
'Too real for you, was it?' sneered
The Great Pozzo. He put the box away.
'Never mind! On with the show!'

'What do you think of it?' Sam whispered
to Liz.

'I don't know,' said Liz.
'It's weird.'

The Great Pozzo looked at her sharply.
Then that look of pain crossed his face again.
He put his hand to his chest.
He breathed hard.

After a minute, the pain seemed to pass.
'On with the show,' he said again.
'Let's have another look in my top hat.
I wonder what we'll find this time?'

6

'I Don't Like it'

The Great Pozzo reached into his top hat.
'What's this?' he said.
'What have we here?'

He pulled out the lobster again.
But this time it was dead.
It was bright red. It had been cooked.
'Magic!' said the Great Pozzo.
'As I said, that's my supper sorted.'

'I don't like this,' Liz said to Sam.
She had a soft spot for animals.
Even lobsters.

The Great Pozzo must have had
very sharp ears.
He turned his head
and stared hard at Liz.
He suddenly looked very angry.
'You don't like it?
And what about me –
do you think I like this?

A man of my talents –
working in this dirty little hole of a place,
doing tricks for a bunch of
ignorant apes like you?
You think I like it?
I'm an old man. I'm not well.
You think I like getting up
on this horrible little stage every night?
Do you think I'd do this
if I didn't have to?
If I didn't need the money to live,
do you think I'd be here?'

There was a long silence.
The audience shifted uneasily.
Liz felt her face going red.

Then the Great Pozzo
seemed to lose all his energy.
He stopped looking angry.

He looked simply tired instead.
'All right,' he said, more quietly.
'Let's get on with it.
On with the show.
For my next trick, I need a lady
from the audience.'

He pointed at Liz.
'You. Lady who doesn't like it.
Come up here and help me.'

Liz looked at Sam.
'What shall I do?'

'Go on,' said Sam.
'Go and help him. It'll be OK.'

Liz got up.
Slowly, she walked to the front.
Slowly, she went up the steps
that led to the tiny stage.

7

The Lady Vanishes

'For my next trick,
I'm going to make you disappear,'
said the Great Pozzo.

At the back of the stage was a tall, thin box,
like a skinny wardrobe.
It was red, with yellow stars and moons
painted on it.
The Great Pozzo pushed it to the front.
The effort made him breathe hard.
Again, that look of pain
crossed his face.
He opened the door of the box.

He tapped the inside with his wand.
'As you see, completely empty.
Now, if this lady would be kind enough
to step inside . . .'

Liz turned and smiled nervously at Sam.
Then she stepped into the box.
The Great Pozzo shut the door.
'Now for the magic words.'
He said some strange words
in a strange language.
He waved his hands in the air.
Then he flung open the door.

The box was completely empty.
The audience clapped.
'As you see, she's gone.
Where has she gone?
Perhaps she'll tell us all about it
when she comes back.
To bring her back,

I need only say some more magic words . . .'

He waved his hands again.
He opened his mouth to say the words –
but then something happened.

The look of pain crossed his face.
He grabbed his chest and bent over.
He was fighting to breathe.
Then he fell on the stage.

8

A Heart Attack

Sam jumped to his feet.
'Can't someone help?
Is there a doctor here?'

'I'm a nurse,' said a young woman.
She jumped on to the stage.
She bent over The Great Pozzo.
'Looks like he's had a heart attack.
Someone call an ambulance!'

She started pushing hard on his chest.
Again and again she pushed.
Nothing happened.
She gave him the kiss of life.
But it was too late.
At last she stood up.
'He's dead,' she said.
She covered his face with his cloak.

'What a nightmare!' thought Sam.
'Poor old Pozzo.
What a way to go.
And poor Liz.
It can't have been very nice for her.'

Sam got up on to the stage.
'Liz,' he said.
'You'd better come out now.'
There was no answer from the box.

9
Where is Liz?

Sam opened the box.

It was empty.

'There must be a false back,' thought Sam.

He tapped on the wood.

'Liz? Where are you?'

There was still no answer.

Sam went round to the back of the box
and tapped again.

'Liz? Don't mess about.

This isn't the time.

Come on.'

There was still no answer.

Sam began to feel scared.
What if she had really disappeared?
No, that was silly . . .
He shook the box hard.
'Come on, Liz! Speak to me!'

He shook the box so hard
that it fell over with a crash.
But there was still no sound from Liz.

Then Sam lost control.
He started to hit and kick the box
with all his strength.
The door came off.
The sides caved in.
In a few minutes,
the box was smashed to pieces.
But there was still no sign of Liz.

Sam stood there on the stage,
not knowing what to do.

Everyone in the theatre helped him look.
So did the police, when they turned up.
But they couldn't find Liz.

'Where's she gone?' Sam kept asking
But no-one could answer.
Wherever Liz had gone, it was somewhere
that people don't come back from.

Sam never saw her again, as long as he lived.